Ways to live a luxurious life

Simple things you need to do to achieve your desired luxurious life

By

Mary Gibson

Table of contents

Introduction

Not only the wealthy and famous may enjoy luxury. Here's how to enjoy a luxurious lifestyle on a small budget.

Americans enjoy luxury, making the country a significant market for high-end products including apparel, accessories, jewelry, and cosmetics.

Although everyone has an own concept of luxury and what it means to live luxuriously, it typically entails blowing your budget on something special: a pricy purse, a spa weekend, supper at a well regarded restaurant, or an international trip. You see what I mean.

However, living in luxury need not entail disregarding your spending plan entirely. You may enjoy a lavish lifestyle without breaking the bank.

Chapter 1
Living in luxury

A luxurious lifestyle includes things like good comfort, a stress-free existence, and genuine happiness. However, keep in mind that maintaining a luxurious lifestyle is expensive. As a result, you can indulge in any sort of entertainment, travel in style, or party with your friends wherever and whenever you want. There are many options available today for leading a happy life. Investing in fashionable clothing, renting a yacht for a party or vacation, purchasing a nice apartment where you will spend more time, and carrying out a number of other actions are all examples of things you may do to achieve the greatest results.

Here are some pointers to help you get started leading a lavish lifestyle; you can also visit their website for more details.

residing in an upscale apartment

It's a good idea to live a rich lifestyle in a contemporary, opulent apartment. Get the best location to search for luxury condominiums that mix comfort and safety if you're seeking for a cutting-edge approach to modern living. When you visit a luxury apartment, you get to appreciate a space that has been painstakingly designed and meant for a life well lived.

Because of this, you can benefit from spacious interiors, swimming at dusk, cocktail hours on the building's rooftop, and easy access to regional music and art. Spending your vacation in the most luxurious locations is another way to enjoy a luxurious lifestyle in addition to renting a nice property for a day or two.

Elect the ideal vacation.

You've really visited a number of significant megacity sails and ocean disquisition spots. Cycling is one of the stylish ways to get outdoors. Living a more opulent life than all these bells and hisses covers all angles of big and small trips. Bike and wildlife suckers frequently propose cycling through the woods.On the stylish megacity's biking paths, you may also enjoy mountain biking. Purchase upmarket luggage to distinguish oneself as a sapient rubberneck. The stylish apparel from the stylish contrivers fits you comfortably.

For contemporary excursionists, there's handcrafted, elaborate leather trolley luggage available.

Time Administration That Works

The distinction between living a lavish lifestyle and overspending your money is quality time. You can purchase anything you desire, such as designer handbags, exquisite jewelry, expensive tuxedos, and possibly a five-star hotel for your opulent getaway. All of this, however, is useless if your business affairs do not provide you peace of mind. Make the most of your comfortable living as a consequence by scheduling your time wisely. There is a proper time for everything, and the following advice will enable you to utilize your time effectively

Put a smartwatch on.

Your benefit from wearing a smartwatch can be enormous.

While away from your laptop or phone, you can still be aware of emails, incoming calls, and messages so that you can stay current. To avoid missing a deadline, you can also email important reminders using your smartwatch.

time management

Utilizing time management tools run by your secretary or personal assistant, you can organize your schedule. As a result, you may better manage your time and only schedule meetings with those who are absolutely necessary. Examine their website before going there. Additionally, you can assign tasks using time management software based on their importance and urgency. This enables you to order jobs by significance and urgency or move them up the priority list.

Chapter 2

11 Ways to Live a Luxurious Life Regardless of Your Budget

an excellent life. We all aspire to it, but what does it entail in practice? For some people, it might entail traveling and interacting with diverse cultures. Others can view it as owning expensive furnishings and clothing. Regardless of what luxury means to you, these lifestyle tips can help you enjoy it to the maximum!

Advice for Living Luxuriously on Any Budget

Most people associate luxury with expensive goods and extravagant lifestyles. However, the reality is that there are numerous ways to live a lavish lifestyle without breaking the bank.

Eleven suggestions for living a lavish life on any budget are provided in this article. Continue reading if you want to learn how to live a little more opulently or if you just want to reward yourself!

1. Buy high- quality items.

Quality is essential when it comes to luxury goods. Investing in high- quality products will make them endure longer and ameliorate over time. also, you'll be suitable to use them for numerous years.Why not make an investment in some precious accessories if you want to add a little fineness to your daily life? Men's dress shoes, a beautiful handbag, a fund forecourt, and nice watches can all significantly ameliorate anensemble.It's respectable to indulge yourself to commodity opulent sometimes. Just make sure it does not bring too much money.

A swish Franck Muller watch

2. Establish an opulent home environmentIt's not necessary to spend a lot of money to have a magnificent home. It only needs to be cozy and soothing.Make your house a reflection of your individuality. You'll feel more at ease and comfortable in your home when it's designed the way you want.

Make your living area feel special by adding opulent accents like fine furniture, fragrant flowers, cozy lighting, or tropical design. Consider using all of your senses while at home. This might be done with fragrant candles, wind chimes, and velvet blankets that are lovely to look at and touch.
To create the minimalist look you see in boutique hotels, reduce clutter. In order to worry less about your belongings while you're gone, having a smart house with cutting-edge security systems is another aspect of living in luxury.
a lavish living room with gold and green decor

3. Create a plan for the lifestyle you desire
Setting up and adhering to a budget is a smart idea. You are less inclined to overspend on useless products when you have a predetermined spending limit. Make sure to put savings in your budget as well!

If you're a more visual person, make a list of your goals and a vision board or money mantras as well. You can either show a physical duplicate of it offline, such as on your refrigerator door, or online. A useful free tool for organizing various mood boards is Pinterest.

You'll be held responsible and motivated as a result. Your objectives should be both attainable and reasonable.

4. Maintain an Active Lifestyle

To feel your best, you need to have a healthy lifestyle. Make sure to exercise frequently and maintain a healthy, balanced diet. You'll feel and look your best thanks to this!

Start juicing now for the best outcomes. It's a fantastic technique to improve the amount of fruit and veggies you consume.

For the optimum quality of life, good mental health is equally crucial. If you're overloaded, try a mental cleanse or utilize a meditation app.

Even if it's cloudy outside, make an effort to get outside every day in the morning. You feel more awake in the morning sun, which also improves the quality of your sleep at night.
We are aware from personal experience how simple it is to develop poor habits and stay up late. The quality of your sleep will be much improved if you can get to bed before midnight. healthy juice beverage

5. Explore the World

Traveling is one of the best ways to discover new cultures and escape the monotony of daily life. Try to travel at least once a year if you can.
Luxury travel encompasses more than simply big boats and private jets. Go island hopping, ask the locals where the best street cuisine can be found, and have a massage on the beach for the best trip memories. You'll return feeling energized and renewed!
To receive notification about ticket sales in advance, sign up for your preferred airline's

marketing emails. Traveling off-peak is one of the finest ways to live a lavish lifestyle on a budget.

You'll not only avoid the crowds but also spend less on your hotel and airfare. Just make sure to research your destination's busiest travel times so you can make the appropriate plans.
Going on islands in Thailand
Why not take a break from your typical routine and enjoy a relaxing staycation? If you're on a tight budget or simply don't want to travel too far, this is a great option. Reserve a room at a posh resort or hotel in the area and treat yourself this weekend. Many of the on-site amenities, like the restaurants, spas, and swimming pools, are also available to you.

6. **As an alternative, think about renting a luxurious holiday home.**
These homes offer all the conveniences of a luxury hotel but frequently have more room and seclusion.

When traveling in a big group, they can also be a wonderful deal.

A fascinating alternative for folks on a tight budget is house swapping. They are available everywhere, but unless you are exchanging keys with someone you already know and trust, utilize a trustworthy agency.

Make the most of your free time with these six luxury travel tips.

If you can, engage in expensive pastimes. This could entail attending cooking classes at a five-star hotel, going skiing or golfing on the weekends, or even hiring a personal trainer to help you keep in shape.

Make a schedule for your work and free time each day. You will feel more organized and effective if you have a routine. Having certain periods set out for unwinding and engaging in your interests can also be beneficial.

your pastimes.

As much time as you can, spend with those you love. One of the best ways to appreciate life is to spend quality time with loved ones.

7. Dress Effortlessly

It's not always expensive to dress elegantly. Just concentrate on making long-lasting purchases of high-quality things. It's simple to create your own distinctive appearance by fusing items from thrift stores and designer labels like Louis Vuitton. Additionally, dressing for your body shape is important. Choose a smart-casual outfit for your flight and a more formal look for special occasions. Construct a small wardrobe. It's simpler to put together outfits and mix and match different pieces when your wardrobe is smaller. It also encourages you to pay more attention to the items you purchase.

An elegant, smart-casual ensemble

8. Relish Luxurious Spa Services

Booking a spa day is another excellent option to indulge in some luxury without spending a lot of money. Numerous local spas provide fantastic discounts on massages, facials, and other services. And why not schedule a mani/pedi if you truly want to spoil yourself? You'll leave feeling renewed and energized!

Spend money on a home hair spa or a steam facial with a few drops of your preferred essential oils for people who are tight on cash. Social media sites like YouTube and TikTok provide some excellent advice. A lavish spa experience

9. Treat Yourself to Luxurious Skincare Items

The best approach to treat oneself is with high-end skincare and cosmetics. The best brands have ingredients that are very effective and have lovely packaging.

They don't have to be extremely expensive either. Both men and women can benefit from using these fantastic mid-range French skincare goods.

Embryolisse, Eucerin, La Roche-Posay, Avène, and Vichy Laboratories are a few of our top online picks. Although they don't come in elegant packaging, they provide amazing hydration at affordable costs. To feel your best, try applying a high-end beauty product at least once a week!

A jade roller and gua sha - great for depuffing

10. Take in some elegant music

For each occasion, luxurious music can create the ideal atmosphere. Whether you're entertaining guests or unwinding at home, pick some opulent music to set the mood.

It might be Mozartian classical music, gentle jazz, or relaxing tunes from Ibiza. Whatever you pick, the most important thing is that it calms you down and improves your mood.

11. **Appreciate opulent experiences**

Spend money on experiences like vacations, shows, and fancy restaurants rather than new goods. More memories will be created by experiences than by a brand-new piece of jewelry. The only way to appreciate luxury is to really live it. Be sure to sample a variety of opulent extras including exquisite meals, wine tastings, and water sports.

You'll be astounded by how delightful and calming they can be! If you're on a tight budget, think about ordering high-end catered in or using a restaurant discount app like Spotluck.

Utilizing free events in your neighborhood is another way to live a lavish lifestyle on a tight budget. Numerous free activities are frequently offered, ranging from concerts and art exhibits to food festivals and block parties. To find out what's going on in your neighborhood, be sure to look in your neighborhood newspaper or online event listings.

Schedule some alone time. Make sure to set aside time each day for yourself, whether it be a soothing bath or reading your favorite book. These kinds of minor details are what really count.

An experience at a fine-dining restaurant Luxury Lifestyle Advice

We can assist if you're looking for methods to live luxuriously on any budget. We provide lifestyle advice that is practical for everyone who is dedicated to living a happy life, regardless of their financial status.

There are many easy ways to live a luxurious life without going broke, from budgeting your money and investing in yourself to appreciating every moment of your day.

The wealthiest individuals understand that having fulfilling relationships and self-assurance are equally crucial to living a life of luxury.

10 Easy Ways To Live A More Luxurious Lifestyle

After a long day at the workplace, you're now lounging in your apartment in whatever city you happen to be in. You notice the mound of laundry that has been glaring back at you for the past four days while you are tired and beginning to become hungry. You're lounging on your living room couch, surfing through social media, and silently following online celebrities who appear to be enjoying the good life at luxurious resorts and far-off locales. You imagine creating your own lavish lifestyle, but it seems so far from being a reality.

Additionally, the laundry won't get done by itself. As a result, you did what any female millennial would do and searched on Google for tips on how to live a slightly more opulent life. Suddenly, you find yourself on this page. Your daydreaming is cut short by the growling of your stomach, which serves as a gentle reminder that you still need to eat. You place a last-minute takeout order since it's too late to prepare. The good news is that you now have 30 minutes before your food is delivered. So relax, pour yourself a glass of wine, and read on to learn how you can find your own version of luxury—not as far off as you might think! Curious

Read on to learn how.

10 Ideas for Luxurious Living

Enjoy the simple pleasures and remember that luxury is a state of mind.

Quality preceding quantity

- Relationships Are Important
- Tighten Up Your Schedule
- Time Limit
- Give comfort and convenience top priority.
- Appreciate the value of leading a healthy lifestyle
- Keep those in need in mind

Take a step back and give it some serious thought before moving on to how you might have a luxurious existence.

The idea of luxury is quite subjective; the individual sitting next to you on the train might not share your definition of luxury. Contrary to popular belief, luxury has more to do with happiness and fulfillment than it does with net value.

In actuality, leading a rich lifestyle involves discovering inner tranquility and contentment with your own life and surroundings. It's a sensation, the sensation that you are living your life to the fullest and nothing less!
Here are some starting considerations: what motivates you to wake up in the morning.
What causes you to feel content? Happy?
Conversely, consider what is now bothering you in your life. Are they unwise practices?
People who no longer support your mentality? Or is it just because you're employed in a job you detest?
Maybe you enjoy your work, but you'd like to enjoy your personal life more.

Your ideas may already be racing at this point, which is fantastic! To build on that, this article aims to demonstrate 10 straightforward ways you can live a more opulent lifestyle. It emphasizes the importance of quality over quantity rather than endless vacations and unlimited champagne. It not only emphasizes self-worth as opposed to net worth, but it also provides advice on how to travel more, maintain physical and mental health, and spruce up your wardrobe without breaking the bank.

Having money is a state of mind

Finding the positives in your own life and really savoring them is the essence of luxury. There will always be room for growth in terms of what you can do, earn, and own, but if you're continuously striving for more without showing gratitude for what you already have, it will all be for naught.

Enjoy the Little Things

Finding ordinary delights in your own house is so simple today! Find luxury in a night in front of the TV with a glass of great wine, find joy in nighttime strolls, and value family time.

Have no ideas? Why not begin a nighttime skin care routine prior to going to bed. You wouldn't believe it, but it doesn't have to be expensive anymore! It is incredible how uplifting it is to pamper oneself before going to bed, and brands like Paula's Choice and The Ordinary provide cheap products that genuinely work. Give yourself a lymphatic drainage facial massage to make it even more opulent. You can find many instructional videos on YouTube for this.

Superior quality to quantity

Investing in high-quality items that will last a long time is what it means to live a lavish lifestyle rather than flaunting your wealth. It entails giving up on making frequent journeys to the store to buy low-quality stuff in favor of investing less frequently in higher-quality goods.

This idea can be used to describe a wide range of things, including your clothes and house furnishings. The goal is to invest in products of higher quality rather than lower quality so that you do not need to replace them as frequently.

How Important Relationships Are

It may be obvious by now, but having a truly opulent lifestyle is not actually about having a lot of money.

Some things that bring satisfaction in life just cannot be purchased. The relationships you have with your family and friends are almost as vital to your health, which is likely at the top of that list (but we'll talk about that further down).

It's simple to make life much more opulent by preserving positive relationships with your family, friends, and intimate circle of acquaintances. Make connections with individuals around you and call a friend you haven't spoken to in a long time. Never undervalue the importance of having loved ones and close friends that you can count on to cheer you up when you're feeling bad.

Consolidate Your Schedule

It's simple to become overburdened in this day and age with everything going on, including a busy job, travel for both personal and professional reasons, housework, and technology at our fingertips. With all of this activity going on continually, it's critical to sit back and set aside time for activities you genuinely enjoy. Try swapping out one of your monthly to-dos for something you enjoy doing, a reward that gives you time to pamper yourself.

Time Limit

Consider limiting your calendar if you're asking yourself, "How am I supposed to streamline my schedule with so much going on?" Simply described, time blocking is a time management strategy that entails segmenting your day into time blocks. Setting a time limit for a work may help you concentrate on finishing it and make you more aware of going over your allotted allotted time. In order to start spending more time on the activities you truly want to be doing, there are a ton of books and free articles online that offer advice on how to time block efficiently.

Put ease and convenience first

Millennials will be the first to tell you how putting convenience and thus comfort first can make modern living much more opulent. In the simplest terms, it comes down to having what you need, when you need it. living a life that requires little effort to achieve your goals.

Understand the Value of Healthy Living

The definition of luxury living is pretty much leading a healthy lifestyle. In reality, everything else loses importance if you don't take care of your health.
It is actually very possible to live a healthy and wealthy lifestyle, which is typically disregarded in favor of accumulating more worldly possessions.
The benefits of a plant-based diet for health and the benefits of regular yoga practice for mental

wellbeing are things we at Dukes Avenue firmly believe in.

Everyone should follow their own moral convictions, but adopting a better way of life will have such a positive effect that you'll wonder how you ever got by without it! As Warren Buffett famously said, chains of habit are not felt until they are too heavy to break.
Keep those in need in mind

Last but not least, remember to share what you have with others who are less fortunate if you are fortunate enough to already feel like your life could be considered to be quite nice. Help someone in need, give to a charity close to your heart, volunteer your time at a nearby nonprofit, or purchase food for an elderly neighbor. Even though these things may seem insignificant, the good you do for others will eventually return to you, and that is a fairly opulent concept.

Chapter 3

The 11 Best-Paying Jobs in the U.S

The highest-paying employment was found to be in the healthcare industry, and the sector has a very promising future. The U.S. Bureau of Labor Statistics (BLS) predicts that between 2020 and 2030, employment in healthcare vocations would increase by 16%, adding roughly 2.6 million new jobs. According to the organization, this growth "is primarily due to an older population, leading to greater demand for healthcare services"1.

KEY LESSONS

- Several healthcare positions were among the highest-paid professions.
- The top 25 highest-paying professions include 15 jobs in the healthcare industry.
- Outside of the healthcare industry, corporate chief executives earn the most money.
- All employment is expected to rise by an average of 8% between 2020 and 2030.

• Owning your own business or working for yourself will have a big impact on your pay possibilities. Outside of chief executive officers, however, that is not taken into account here (CEOs).

The rankings are based on wage information from the BLS. In the yearly publication, National Occupational Employment and Wage Estimates, the BLS utilizes mean, or average salaries, rather than median earnings for each occupation, which represent the annual wage of a typical employee in that function.

1. Anesthesia professionals: $331,190

Anesthesiologists are medical professionals who "administer anesthetics and analgesics for pain management prior to, during, or after surgery," according to the BLS. The highest paying occupation is this extremely specialized one, according to a recent list.

Anesthesiologists work according to the operating room's timetable, which might be lengthy and unreliable. This is due to the fact that anesthesiologists are required for both routine surgeries and emergency procedures, such as childbirth and traumatic events.

• Education — In the United States, future anesthesiologists typically complete a four-year residency in anesthesiology, and in certain cases even longer programs, depending on the specialization. The BLS predicts that overall employment will decline by 1% between 2020 and 2030.

2. oral and maxillofacial surgeons: $311,460

In and around the mouth and jaw, oral and maxillofacial surgeons treat a variety of illnesses, wounds, and deformities.

Problematic wisdom teeth, misaligned jaws, tumors, and cysts of the jaw and mouth are some of the most frequent issues they're likely to handle. Additionally, they might operate on dental implants.

• Education – Oral and maxillofacial surgeons typically need a bachelor's degree, four years of dental school, and at least four years of residency. The American Board of Oral and Maxillofacial Surgery certified surgeons in the United States once they complete their training by requiring them to pass a two-part test.

• Job Prospects — The BLS predicts that employment will rise by 8% between 2020 and 2030.

3. Doctors of obstetrics and gynecology: $296,210

Obstetricians-gynecologists, often known as OB-GYNs, are medical professionals with a focus on reproductive health and childbirth, and their annual salaries are only somewhat higher than those for general surgeons.

Successful OB-GYNs are skilled in imparting knowledge to patients that enhances both their and their unborn children's health. They also do exceptionally well in high-stress circumstances, most notably childbirth, which might happen at unusual times of the day.

• Education — Becoming an OB-GYN requires graduation from medical school as well as the completion of an obstetrics program and a gynecology residency program, which normally last four years. These medical professionals need to pass a licensing exam after two years of clinical practice.

• Job Prospects — The BLS predicts a 2% decline in OB-GYN employment between 2020 and 2030.

4. Physicians: $294,520

Although it takes years of specialized training to become a surgeon, these elite doctors are rewarded with one of the highest-paying professions.

Depending on their speciality, surgeons could work a lot of erratic hours. While surgeons who focus on routine and elective procedures may have a more predictable schedule, those who specialize in trauma or neurosurgery frequently work long shifts, sometimes even overnight.

Surgeons undertake operations to treat conditions including cancer and shattered bones. Surgeons oversee the patient's postoperative and preoperative treatment. A surgeon may need to speak with a patient on the phone even though they are not scheduled to do so, and on-call surgeons may need to visit a hospital in an emergency.

• Instruction — Successful completion of medical school, a lengthy residency period, and occasionally a specialized fellowship are prerequisites for becoming a surgeon.

• Employment Outlook – From 2020 to 2030, it is predicted that overall employment will grow by 3%.5.

5. Oral surgeons: $267,280

Orthodontists are specialists in dental correction techniques and are frequently recommended by

patients' dentists. These medical professionals regularly take X-rays, put braces on, make mouth guards, and carry out other procedures as necessary.
Since they deal directly with patients, high-achieving orthodontists need to be skilled communicators as well as strong analysts and problem-solvers. Some people own their own practice, which calls for good management skills, while others work for major orthodontic offices.

• Education — Future orthodontists must complete a dental school curriculum that includes both classroom and clinical training after receiving a bachelor's degree. The next step for these recently graduated doctors is to finish a specific residency program and take a license exam.

6. Physicians (Other): $255,110 2020

They would rank sixth if you took the mean salary of all doctors practicing in all other disciplines.

Allergists, cardiologists, dermatologists, oncologists (who treat cancer), gastroenterologists (specialists in the digestive system), and ophthalmologists are among the many professions that fall under this category of "other" (eye specialists). It also includes radiologists, who examine medical images and give radiation therapy to cancer patients, and pathologists, who examine body tissue for any anomalies.

• Education — After earning a bachelor's degree, any medical doctor (M.D.) or doctor of osteopathic medicine (D.O.) must attend medical school. Although some may continue on to acquire fellowship training after that, the majority of clinical professions also demand the successful completion of a resident program.

7. Doctors of psychiatry: $249,760

While all psychiatrists work to treat mental health conditions, there are several different subfields within the practice.

For instance, some specialize in child and adolescent psychiatry, while others focus on forensic (legal), addiction, or consultation psychiatry, which takes place in a medical context. Others focus on psychoanalysis, where the psychiatrist aids the patient in recalling and examining earlier experiences and emotions in order to more fully comprehend their present emotions.
Psychiatrists serve in a variety of settings, including private practice, hospitals, community organizations, schools, treatment centers, and even jails.

• Education – Psychiatrists are medical professionals, not psychologists. They have to complete medical school after getting their undergraduate degree, then a residency program.

. The American Psychiatric Association states that the first year of residency is often spent addressing a variety of medical illnesses in a hospital setting, followed by three or more years devoted to mental health and medication. The American Board of Psychiatry and Neurology certification is then frequently sought after by recent graduates.

• Job Prospects — Over the coming years, one of the medical professions with the quickest growth is anticipated to be psychology. According to the BLS, employment will increase 13% between 2020 and 2030.

8. Doctors of internal medicine: $242,190

Internists specialize in treating adult patients and frequently work as primary care physicians or hospitalists.

As with other general practitioners, internists who work in primary care settings treat a wide range of illnesses, from high cholesterol and hypertension to asthma and diabetes. Quick decision-making abilities are essential due to visits frequently lasting 15 or 30 minutes.

Education — Internists often undergo a residency program where they rotate through various healthcare specializations after graduating from college and passing medical school. Some choose to seek more specialized education in fields including oncology, pulmonology, and cardiology. Board-certified internists have a significant advantage in the job market.

• Employment Trends – The BLS projects a 1% decline in general internist employment between 2020 and 2030.

9. Physicians in family medicine: $235,930

Physicians who" diagnose, treat, and offer precautionary care to individuals and families across the lifetime" are included in this group, according to the BLS. For further advanced medical care, these interpreters constantly shoot their cases to experts. Cases frequently visit family drug croakers , generally pertaining to primary care croakers, for routine checks and the treatment of common ails like sinus and respiratory infections. Some primary care croakers specialize in treating either children or grown-ups(internists)(pediatricians). Family croakers are those who watch for cases of all periods, from babies to the senior. Family practice croakers generally handle a lesser range of medical affections due to their different case demographic.

• Education – Family drug croakers must finish an occupancy program once they've graduated from medical academy. Before submitting an operation for board instrument, croakers must spend a specific quantum of months in each training area.

• Job Outlook The BLS projects a 5 increase in family drug croaker employment between 2020 and 2030.Those in charge$,020 Outside of the medical and dentistry fields, principal directors are the group of people with the loftiest hires. The CEO's duties include leading the establishment into new requests or product lines, interacting with the board of directors, and making important choices regarding the operation platoon.

• Education – Family medicine doctors must finish a residency program once they have graduated from medical school. Before submitting an application for board certification, doctors must spend a specific amount of months in each training area.

• Job Outlook: The BLS projects a 5% increase in family medicine physician employment between 2020 and 2030.

5\s10.

Those in charge: $213,020

The CEO's duties include leading the firm into new markets or product lines, interacting with the board of directors, and making important choices regarding the management team.

Many chief executives have demanding schedules despite being highly paid.

• Education — It is not unexpected that the majority of Fortune 100 CEOs (53%) have a bachelor's degree in business administration, according to a Forbes research. However, a lot of them had majored in unrelated subjects in college (though some later received a master of business administration, or MBA, degree). Many top leaders in tech-related businesses were undergraduate engineers.

• Job Outlook — From 2020 to 2030, it is anticipated that the number of senior executives would increase by roughly 8%.

11. $192,470 for nurse anesthetists.

Compared to most other professions, nursing generally has good compensation, but nurse anesthetists tend to earn more. Nursing anesthesia professionals, according to the BLS, "administer anesthetic and provide care before, during, and after surgical, therapeutic, diagnostic, and obstetrical operations."

Thus, obtaining a nurse anesthesia license requires less time and money than completing a medical education and becoming a doctor. Certified registered nurse anesthetists (CRNAs) can find employment in a wide range of places, such as pain management clinics, obstetrical delivery rooms, ambulatory surgery centers, and hospital operating rooms.

• Education — Applicants must complete a master's degree program that is accredited, which normally lasts 24 to 51 months. Some people continue on to finish a fellowship program, especially if they're specialized in the same area. Candidates must have at least a year of full-time experience as a registered nurse in a critical-care setting in order to become a CRNA.

www.ingramcontent.com/pod-product-compliance
Lightning Source LLC
LaVergne TN
LVHW020526160826
845677LV00015B/3916
9798847183925